TINTIN'S TRAVEL DIARIES

Publisher's note:

Tintin, the intrepid reporter, first made his appearance January 10, 1929, in a serial newspaper strip with an adventure in the Soviet Union. From there, it was on to the Belgian Congo and then to America. Together with his dog, Snowy; an old seaman, Captain Haddock; an eccentric professor, Cuthbert Calculus; look-alike detectives, Thomson and Thompson; and others, Tintin roamed the world from one adventure to the next.

Tintin's dog, Snowy, a small white fox terrier, converses with Tintin, saves his life many times, and acts as his confidant, despite his weakness for whiskey and a tendency toward greediness. Captain Haddock, in some ways Snowy's counterpart, is a reformed lover of whiskey, with a tendency toward colorful language and a desire to be a gentleman-farmer. Cuthbert Calculus, a hard-of-hearing, sentimental, absent-minded professor, goes from small-time inventor to nuclear physicist. The detectives, Thomson and Thompson, stereotyped characters down to their old-fashioned bowler hats and outdated expressions, are always chasing Tintin. Their attempts at dressing in the costume of the place they are in make them stand out all the more.

The Adventures of Tintin appeared in newspapers and books all over the world. Georges Remi (1907–1983), better known as Hergé, based Tintin's adventures on his own interest in and knowledge of places around the world. The stories were often irreverent, frequently political and satirical, and always exciting and humorous.

Tintin's Travel Diaries is a new series, inspired by Hergé's characters and based on notebooks Tintin may have kept as he traveled. Each book in this series takes the reader to a different country, exploring its geography, and the customs, the culture, and the heritage of the people living there. Hergé's original cartooning is used, juxtaposed with photographs showing the country as it is today, to give a feeling of fun as well as education.

If Hergé's cartoons seem somewhat out of place in today's society, think of the time in which they were drawn. The cartoons reflect the thinking of the day, and set next to modern photographs, we learn something about ourselves and society, as well as about the countries Tintin explores. We can see how attitudes have changed over the course of half a century.

Hergé, himself, would change his stories and drawings periodically to reflect the changes in society and the comments his work would receive. For example, when it was originally written in 1930, *Tintin in the Congo*, on which *Tintin's Travel Diaries: Africa* is based, was slanted toward Belgium as the fatherland. When Hergé prepared a color version in 1946, he did away with this slant. Were Hergé alive today, he would probably change many other stereotypes that appear in his work.

From the Congo, Tintin went on to America. This was in 1931. Al Capone was notorious, and the idea of cowboys and Indians, prohibition, the wild west, as well as factories, all held a place of fascination.

Cigars of the Pharaoh (1934) introduced Hergé's fans to the mysteries of India. A trip to China came with *The Blue Lotus* in 1936, the first story Hergé thoroughly researched. After that, everything was researched, including revisions of previous stories.

Tintin's Travel Diaries are fun to read, fun to look at, and provide educational, enjoyable trips around the world. Perhaps, like Tintin, you, too, will be inspired to seek out new adventures!

The publisher particularly wishes to thank Mrs. Christine Ockrent and television channel Antenne 2 for their kind permission to use the title *Travel Diaries*.

TINTIN'S TRAVEL DIARIES

A collection conceived and produced by Martine Noblet.

Les films du sable thank the following the following **Connaissance du monde** photographers for their participation in this work:

Olivier Berthelot, Emmanuel Braquet, Jean-Noel de Golish, Patrick Moreau, Jean Ratel.

The authors thank D. De Bruyker and C. Erard for their collabration.

First edition for the United States and Canada published by Barron's Educational Series, Inc., 1994.

All inquiries should be addressed to:
Barron's Educational Series, Inc.
250 Wireless Boulevard
Hauppauge, New York 11788

Library of Congress Catalog Card No.: 94-13754

International Standard Book No. 0-8120-6427-5 (hardcover)
International Standard Book No. 0-8120-1866-4 (paperback)

Library of Congress Cataloging-in-Publication Data

Braquet, Anne.
    [Carnets de route de Tintin, India. English]
    Tintin's travel diaries, India / text by Anne Braquet,
Martine Noblet ; translation by Maureen Walker.
        p. cm.
    A collection conceived and produced by Martine Noblet.
    Includes bibliographical reference and index
    ISBN 0-8120-6427-5 (cloth). — ISBN 0-8120-1866-4 (paper)
1. India—Description and trave—Juvenile literature.
[1. India. 2. Cartoons and comics.] I. Noblet, Martine.
Carnets de route de Tintin, India. English. II. Title
DS414.2.B7213   1994
915.404—dc20   94-13754
                                                           CIP
                                                           AC

PRINTED IN HONG KONG
4567 9927 987654321

INDIA

Text by Anne Braquet, Martine Noblet

Translation by Maureen Walker

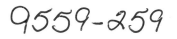

9559-259

BARRON'S

I met Tintin for the first time in the Congo. I must have been about eight years old, the most heroic of ages. As a budding explorer, I considered my backyard a jungle and the placid tomcats who prowled around there ferocious tigers, and Snowy wasn't even there to warn me when they would attack!

I invented some terrifying adventures for myself.

As soon as I got to know him, Tintin became a big brother—distant and inaccessible, but still a big brother. Both of us were adventurers, you understand—he in every continent; I in my backyard. The world was really a pretty good place. So you can imagine how pleased I was, much later, to run into Tintin in a teahouse in Katmandhu, Nepal. I jumped at the opportunity to tell him how much I thought of him, and all the dreams he had inspired in my childhood imagination, and how it helped me to escape from the real adult world. I think he understood, but our paths were taking different directions. He was off to rescue a friend who had been taken prisoner by the Yeti and I was on my way to film the last tigers in Terai—real tigers, this time, in a real jungle! Since then, we have seen each other again many times, and I am happy to accompany him now to India. The big brother is neither distant nor inaccessible now.

And I like it that way.

EMMANUEL BRAQUET

The Tintin books were my first "travel guides."

From the age of 10, often sitting on a doorstep, at a friend's house, or just tucked into bed, I traveled the big cartoon pages, searching the brightly colored frames for details foreign to me.

Sometimes, in the features of Tintin the adventurer-reporter, I seemed to see my father, who was exploring India at the time. Sometimes Hergé's hero, in my young mind, was helping him discover mysterious places and forgotten temples.

My many adventures in India, a country that has become my special field of expertise and, in a way, my workplace, have never made me forget the Maharaja of Rawhajpoutalah in *Cigars of the Pharaoh*, Shiva Dancing, the Fakir, Captain Haddock, Cuthbert Calculus, or any other friend of Tintin, the hero who left his mark on our hearts as children, adolescents, and even adults.

JEAN-NOEL DE GOLISH

TOOOOT

CONTENTS

Words in **heavy** type in the text refer to the glossary beginning on page 70.

WHAT ARE INDIA'S NATURAL BORDERS?

Although it is connected to Asia, India is actually separate from it on the north by the highest mountains in the world. It is an immense subcontinent, a world apart, unlike any other....

The triangular-shaped Indian **peninsula** has not always been part of Asia. Millions of years ago it formed, along with the island of Madagascar and Australia, a continent that no longer exists. When the continent broke up, the part that was to become India slowly drifted northward, and came to rest against the continent of Asia. The world's highest mountain ranges—the Himalaya, the Pamir, and Karakoram—resulted from this collision. These gigantic natural barriers shelter India from the severe climate of Central Asia.

Protected by its mountainous ramparts, the **subcontinent** (one-third the size of the United States) is made up of people who have been able to preserve their own languages, religions, and cultures, associated with an ancient way of life. A few mountain passes provided the only way of getting through the Himalaya mountain range, thus enabling waves of invaders over the years to conquer it.

The first invaders were nomadic tribes of **Aryans,** from which some present-day Indians are descended. In the Middle Ages, Islamic conquerors were followed by **Mongol hordes.** They settled mainly in the immense fertile plain—the North Indian Plain—where three great rivers flow: the Ganges, the Indus (in what is now Pakistan), and, the Brahmaputra. Eventually, the plain joins the large Thar Desert in northwestern India. Cut off from their native land by the mountains through which they had made their way, invaders eventually adopted the way of life of the Indians. To the South, the ancient rocky Deccan plateau of the **peninsula** is harder to reach. It is still inhabited today by the descendants of the first inhabitants of India—the **Dravidians.**

Top: Young Indian woman
Bottom: View of the Himalayas

SHOULD WE SAY "INDIAN" OR "HINDU"?

Indians are the inhabitants of India; there are currently over 850 million of them. Of these, 83 percent practice a religion known as Hinduism.

They are called Hindus....

In 1942, when Christopher Columbus landed in what is today the West Indies, he thought that he had reached the coast of India. Indeed, he was hoping to find a westward route to India across the Atlantic Ocean. At the time there were two routes to the Indies: by sea, around Africa, or by land, crossing the Arab countries of the Middle East.

Because of Columbus' misconception, the inhabitants of the new land were called "Indians." Actually, the only true Indians are the inhabitants of India. What was formerly called the "Indies" now comprises four countries: Pakistan and Bangladesh, essentially **Muslim**, Sri Lanka—formerly Ceylon—which is mainly **Buddhist**, and India itself, the largest and most heavily populated of these states, whose inhabitants are still faithful to the Hindu religion.

Indians have always been deeply interested in spiritual life, and they practice a number of religions. There are over 700 million Hindus and almost 100 million Muslims in India, as well as Christians, Jews, **Sikhs**, **Parsis**, and **Jains**.... The diversity of beliefs sometimes leads to very violent feuds. In spite of their differences, however, and in addition to great religious fervor, all Indians share the same customs and the same brilliant and highly colorful lifestyle.

Top: Indian
Bottom: Minarets on a mosque in Kashmir

WHY DO HINDUS WORSHIP SEVERAL GODS?

3

According to the Hindu religion, God is present in every element of creation. He may be worshipped in many different names, and also in the form of a star, an animal, a flower....

There is no one founder of Hinduism, as there is in Christianity and Islam, and, for Hindus, the creator is not separate from his creation. God is not imagined as a separate person. He is manifest in everything that exists. He "is" the sky, sun, stars, rain, fire, plants, animals, and man, for He is present in every animal and every thing. For a Hindu, it would be wrong to not respect the divine presence, in himself as well as in everything around him.

Hindus also believe in reincarnation, in which the soul never dies but, when a person dies, his soul returns to the world in another form, human or animal, nobler or more lowly, depending on the good or bad deeds he performed in his previous life. The destiny determined by these past actions is called "karma," which means "to do."

To evoke the mystery of life, three "countenances" are attributed to God: When he creates the world, he is Brahma; when he supports it, he is called Vishnu; when he destroys it to recreate it, his name becomes Shiva. The three countenances themselves are subject to successive incarnations. Thus they are known and venerated in a multitude of forms and names, which vary from one region to another. Each of the divine incarnations has its adherents and its temples. Priests known as Brahmans make various offerings at the temples three or four times a day: food, flowers, music....

Right: Woman praying

Above: Detail of a Hindu temple

WHAT IS AN "UNTOUCHABLE"?

The "Untouchables," or Pariahs, are Hindus who do not belong to any of the castes making up Hindu society. Members of the castes always considered them to be unclean.

According to the sacred texts of the Vedas—the Hindu "Bible"—human beings were born from various parts of the body of Brahma, the creator-god. Their descendants belong to different social classes called **castes**. The highest caste members are the Brahmans, said to be born from Brahma's mouth. Even today, many members of this caste are eminent scholars or priests. Then comes the Kshatriya, the caste of kings and warriors, born from Brahma's arms. The Vaisya, who sprang from his thighs, are farmers, professionals, and merchants. The Sudra, born from his feet, are menial servants. The Pariahs were considered unclean because they were not born from the body of Brahma, but emerged from the earth. Thus they were excluded from the four traditional castes.

Each caste lives more or less reclusively, observing its own customs and its own restrictions on foods. Since the Pariahs had no restrictions, they were able to cut and eat the flesh of dead animals, dress hides, clean up garbage and excrement, or drink alcohol—all activities that are considered unclean by Hindus. For this reason, Pariahs were "untouchable," and those Hindus who went near them were obliged to undertake lengthy purifying rites.

In 1950 the country's constitution made it illegal for a person to be considered an Untouchable. Although the government has spent millions of dollars to provide education and jobs for them, discrimination against them still exists, especially in rural areas.

Right:
Untouchable women

Above: Untouchables gathering camel manure in Pushkar

WHY ARE THERE SO MANY FESTIVALS IN INDIA?

Throughout the country, all year long, Indians honor the gods of their various religions with countless festivals and with pilgrimages.

Except for Republic Day, on January 26, Independence Day on August 15, and Mahatma Gandhi's birthday on October 2, all the important festivals are connected with some religion—Hindu, Muslim, Jainism, etc. The Hindu festivals are the most numerous and the largest. The majority of them follow the cycles of nature, celebrating the moon or the sun, the harvest, the return of the **monsoon**, the end of winter, or the arrival of the first flowers. There are other festivals as well—one for women, for instance, and even one for snakes.

Some festivities take place in private, within the family; others take place at the temple. In addition to prayers, offerings, and ritual bathing, during which the faithful are purified, celebrations often include a procession with a statue or a flower-decked elephant that is brought to the bathing pool accompanied by music and sacred dances.

Although some festivals are limited to one city or one region, the principal ones are celebrated all over the country. For instance, during Diwali, the happiest Hindu festival, which comes in late October and early November, all of India is lit with small oil lamps set in the windows and in front of the houses in honor of Lakshmi, the Hindu Goddess of Prosperity. Both Hindus and Muslims make many pilgrimages—visits to holy places. Hindus travel to the Ganges River to bathe there; Muslims visit their shrines.

Festival in Trichūr for Shiva and Vishnu

ARE SADHUS, YOGIS, AND FAKIRS MAGICIANS?

To some extent, the fakir is regarded as a magician who performs tricks at fairs. Yogis and sadhus devote their bodies to spiritual and religious ends.

Religion in India is an essential part of life. In addition to the Brahmans, the Hindu priests who say prayers and make offerings in the temples, there are the **hermits** and sadhus, who renounce material life to devote themselves to their souls. They have no home, no money, and no family. Some of them even go without clothes and try to drive out of their hearts all the passions that link them to the world, even love. They subsist on the charity of the faithful. In this way they will attain their goal, which is to be freed from the reincarnation cycle and soon reach **Nirvana**, the Paradise of the Hindu.

The yogis practice Hinduism. They live a very pure life devoted to physical exercise and meditation. Subjected to the harshest deprivation, they have acquired great wisdom and an extraordinary ability to control their bodies. They can go a long time without eating, sleeping, or even breathing.

Unlike the sadhus and the yogis, the fakirs, whose religion is Islam, are generally less well regarded by Indians. They do in fact use their bodies to earn money. Through work and concentration, they train themselves to not feel pain. They are able to swallow glowing coals, sit on a board with pointed nails sticking through it, or even charm a cobra.

Top: Yogi in Varanasi
Bottom and left: Sadhu

WHY DO HINDUS BATHE IN THE GANGES?

To the Hindus, the Ganges is a sacred river, because its waters are said to purify everything they touch. Dying in a state of purity means one can hope for a better reincarnation....

Hindus long to not be born again after death, for every life, even happy and prosperous, is a burden compared to nirvana, the Hindu paradise, in which the soul blends peacefully into the universe. Therefore, throughout life, Hindus make offerings to the gods, purify themselves every day, and make long pilgrimages to famous temples or sacred mountains or lakes. The surest way to avoid returning to earth, and thus to reach nirvana, is to die on the banks of the Ganges, in Varanasi, if possible.

Varanasi (Benares) is India's holiest city. Every year, over a million Hindus go there on pilgrimages to pray and to bathe in the Ganges. Many devout people, when they feel that death is at hand, ask to have their bodies cremated on the banks of the sacred river and their ashes scattered on its waters.... Then Shiva, the great god of Benares, will reveal to their souls the holy words that will permit them to enter into paradise.

In order to await death in comfort and to die in piety, wealthy **maharajas** built sumptuous palaces and fine temples on the banks of the sacred river.

Religious washing at the Ganges in Varanasi

WHY ARE COWS SACRED TO HINDUS?

Children have always needed milk to grow strong and healthy. Since the cow gives milk, it has become the symbol of everything good and gentle in the universe. To kill it is considered a sacrilege.

Travelers to India are always surprised to see cows browsing on public lawns in total freedom, wandering the streets, or dozing in the middle of crossroads. Rather than disturbing the peaceful animals, drivers prefer to wait until they leave voluntarily.

In India, cows are often better treated than human beings; everyone looks after them and feeds them without regard for the expense. In Benares, the holy city, there is even a hospice for aged cows! But why is so much care taken of these animals, since killing them for food is forbidden?

When the Indians' ancestors arrived in India, their herds were their only valuable possessions. The nutritious cows' milk was the children's only protection from frequent famine. Therefore, killing the precious animals was forbidden, as much out of prudence in case of a food shortage as out of respect for this symbol of maternal gentleness and generosity.

Sacred cows

WHAT IS CREMATION?

In India, only Muslims bury their dead. Hindus burn them respectfully on a funeral pyre, then scatter their ashes on the waters of a river. The process is called cremation....

When the body of the deceased is to be cremated, it is carefully washed and perfumed. It is then wrapped in brightly colored fabric and adorned with garlands of flowers. The mourners chant prayers as they carry the body on a litter to the pyre, traditionally constructed on the banks of a river. The deceased's nearest relative—generally the eldest son, for the widow stays at home with the hired mourners—then lights the pyre. For this he will often use the sacred fire that burns continuously in the home and symbolizes the soul of the family.

The family will have taken care to buy plenty of wood—ideally, the delicately perfumed sandalwood—so that the deceased, purified by the flames and completely reduced to ashes, may join one of the seven sacred rivers in India and be dissolved in the world....

In the past, some Hindu wives, for love of their dead husbands (or for fear of being tormented by their in-laws), threw themselves into the flames alive, to be burned along with their beloved. This custom was called *sati*. It was declared illegal in 1829 but continued through the 1800s. It is rarely seen today.

Left: Funeral offerings
Above: Funeral pyre on a river

WHAT HAPPENS AT A MARRIAGE CEREMONY IN INDIA?

Even today, young Indian men and women do not choose their spouses or the date of their wedding; their families make the decisions for them. The day of the ceremony is set by astrologers and is the occasion for great rejoicing.

Many parents arrange marriages for their children when they are very young. The marriage is always within their caste. Most young people submit to this choice, for fear of opposing their parents, or becoming "unclean," like the Untouchables, if they marry outside their caste. They are not even free to set the wedding date. This choice is reserved for the astrologers, so that the union may occur under a lucky star, ensuring happiness and prosperity.

A daughter's wedding is a great expense for her parents. They must pay so large a dowry that they may be in debt for the rest of their lives. If their house is not large enough or grand enough for the occasion, they have to rent a hall. Finally, and this is true even for poor people, the bride must be adorned like a princess, covered with jewelry, and dressed in a crimson **sari** embroidered with gold thread.

The ceremony never varies: A priest recites the sacred texts and guides certain ritualistic gestures that the future spouses must perform. Only when the wedding is concluded may the husband uncover his wife's face, by lifting the veil that has hidden it. The many relatives and friends invited to the wedding file past the couple, congratulating them. In addition to a gift, each one gives the bride and groom a handful of rice, wishing them as many children as there are grains in it....

Left: Young bride
Right: Marriage ceremony

DO ALL INDIAN CHILDREN GO TO SCHOOL?

In theory, all Indian children between the ages of 5 and 10 must attend school, which is free. More than half of them, however, are too poor to pay for school supplies and books, and are unable to attend....

It is a sad fact that many Indian families are too poor to buy the required school uniform, supplies and books, and therefore do not send their children to school. Also children who are in school can no longer help their parents to earn their meager living. And so, in the country, two out of three children work in the fields. In the cities, two out of five children work, sometimes long hard hours. Without an education, they will be poor all their lives.

In rural India, if there happens to be a teacher to hold classes, school is likely to take place at the corner of the village street, with students sitting on the ground, facing an old black-painted wall that serves as a blackboard! The Indian government is doing its best to improve the situation, and is gradually improving education.

In addition to public schools—for which there are fees when the child is over 10 years old—there are some expensive, private institutions, where families who can afford it send their children. The curricula are demanding; some of the classes are given in English and the passing score in the annual examinations is 70 points out of 100. Girls are the main victims of the education system in India, because preference is given to educating boys. Three out of every four women cannot read or write, because they never went to school.

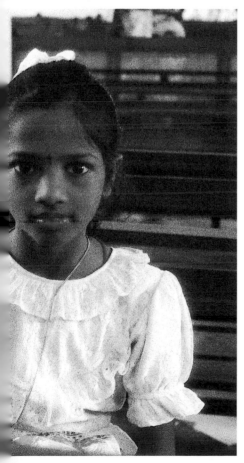

Top: Rural school
Bottom: Young student

DO ALL INDIANS SPEAK THE SAME LANGUAGE?

In India, 16 official languages are spoken, and about 700 to 800 dialects, or local languages! To understand each other, Indians sometimes use Hindi, the language of the northern part of the country, and sometimes English.

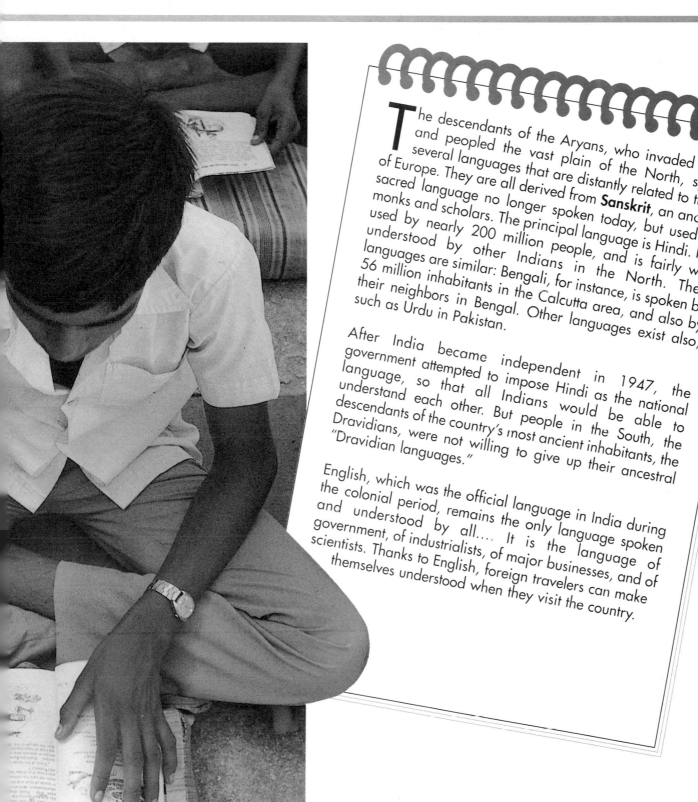

The descendants of the Aryans, who invaded India and peopled the vast plain of the North, speak several languages that are distantly related to those of Europe. They are all derived from **Sanskrit**, an ancient sacred language no longer spoken today, but used by monks and scholars. The principal language is Hindi. It is used by nearly 200 million people, and is fairly well understood by other Indians in the North. Their languages are similar: Bengali, for instance, is spoken by 56 million inhabitants in the Calcutta area, and also by their neighbors in Bengal. Other languages exist also, such as Urdu in Pakistan.

After India became independent in 1947, the government attempted to impose Hindi as the national language, so that all Indians would be able to understand each other. But people in the South, the descendants of the country's most ancient inhabitants, the Dravidians, were not willing to give up their ancestral "Dravidian languages."

English, which was the official language in India during the colonial period, remains the only language spoken and understood by all.... It is the language of government, of industrialists, of major businesses, and of scientists. Thanks to English, foreign travelers can make themselves understood when they visit the country.

Young student learning English

WHAT IS THE FAVORITE ENTERTAINMENT OF INDIANS?

Indians have always loved music, poetry, and the fabulous legends of the gods. Today, in the country as well as in the city, their favorite form of entertainment is the movies.

Every evening 12 million Indians fill the movie theaters, leaving millions more outside, for lack of room. In town, the people crowd into huge air-conditioned halls; in the country, they sit close together in hastily built, open sheds, or in front of simple portable screens erected for one evening on the village square. At every showing there's a scramble to buy a ticket, which costs only a few rupees*, providing access to three hours of daydreams, opening the gates to a universe in which good triumphs over bad, lovers overcome social barriers, and disunited families become reconciled.

Indian movies can sometimes be difficult to follow. The stories are often the same, with tangled plots, and interruptions for dances and songs, which immediately become huge popular hits.

India is one of the foremost film-producing countries—more than 700 a year!—with a single rival—Egypt. Movies are turned out on a production line in studios in Bombay, Madras, Bangalore, or Calcutta. They are often dubbed into various local languages, and the public idolizes the stars as if they were demi-gods!

*1 rupee = three cents

La Déesse

UN FILM DE
SATYAJIT RAY

Top: Scene from the
film "The Goddess"
by Satyajit Ray
Bottom left: Indian
movie house
Bottom right: Poster of the
film "The Goddess"

HOW DO INDIANS DRESS?

In the big cities, many young Indian men follow the western fashion and wear jeans and a shirt. Most women, however, remain faithful to the traditional dress—the sari.

The sari, a light and practical garment, is the favorite dress of Indian women. Around their waists they wrap a piece of fabric that is about six yards long. It hangs to their feet, and they throw the loose end over their left shoulder. Some women wear blouses under the sari. Wealthy women choose gold- or silver-embroidered silk fabric, while the poor make do with plain cotton. Most women wear bracelets and earrings. Though the sari reveals the social status of its wearer, it also supplies information about her region of origin, or events in her life. For instance, a white sari is a sign of mourning, while young brides wear red. In the North, women often wear a long blouse over full trousers.

The *kumkum* is a round dot made of red or black powder that is worn in the middle of a woman's forehead. It is considered a mark of beauty.

Men's clothing is varied. There are still many traditional costumes, which change according to the region. In the North, men wear tunics and jodhpurs—white trousers that are full at the hips and thighs but close-fitting at the ankles. Primarily in the South, many men wear the *dhoti*, the simple white cotton garment wrapped between the legs like loose trousers that was worn long ago by the peasants. Many Hindu men wear turbans. In the cities, most Indian men today often choose to wear lightweight western clothing.

Top: Water carriers in Rajasthan
Bottom left: Group of women talking
Bottom right: Woman in a sari

WHAT DO PEOPLE EAT IN INDIA?

15

Rice is the basic food in India as it is nearly everywhere in Asia. Indians also enjoy spices. Several religions forbid the consumption of meat or alcohol.

Food in India varies according to religion, caste, and income; therefore, it cannot be said that there is one food common to all the country's inhabitants. Jains and Brahmans (the Hindu priests) are not permitted to eat meat or fish; they are strictly vegetarian. Muslims do not eat pork. But the taboo common to all Indians, whatever their caste, is alcohol, and only the Untouchables are allowed to drink it. They are even allowed to eat the meat of sacred cows that have died of old age.

Rice remains the basis of an Indian meal. Served with flat bread called *chapati*, lentils, and vegetables, it is often flavored with spices. *Dal*, a porridge made of pulses (seeds of chickpeas, beans, and lentils) is also eaten with rice and chapatis. Samosas—deep-fried pastries stuffed with potatoes, vegetables, or meat—are popular, as is chicken and lamb that are baked in ovens called *tandoors*. Another popular dish is curry, a spicy stew of vegetables, seafood, or meat. Chutney, a relish made of fruit and spices, often accompanies the meal, and *raita*, a mixture of yogurt and fruit and vegetables, is a cool, refreshing dish. Pepper, cinnamon, and cardamom are popular spices in India. Most Indians drink tea. They enjoy fruits such as watermelon, coconut, and mangoes.

People do not use plates in India—or knives and forks. Food is served on a tray or, in the South, on a banana leaf, and is put into the mouth very neatly after it has been rolled into a ball with the fingers of the right hand.

Left: Preparation of chapatis
Right: Spice Merchant

WHY ARE MONSOONS BOTH THE WORST AND THE BEST OF THINGS?

The monsoon is a seasonal, rain-filled wind. Beginning in June, it showers the dry and overheated land. Heavy rain brings abundant harvests, but if there is too much rain, watch out for floods!

Life in India takes its tempo every year from the rainy season that brings relief from the stifling heat of the summer months. The rains are important because they water the fields sown with seed, and fill the reservoirs. For the rest of the year, these reservoirs will make it possible to irrigate the fields under cultivation and provide drinking water for humans and animals.

From April on, the inhabitants of the South watch for the start of the monsoon, which will spread across every region of the country until October. A good monsoon, which starts in time to water the crops and replenish water supplies, is the promise of abundant harvests....

Unfortunately, the monsoon is a changeable climatic phenomenon. If the rains are too light, a drought results that will rage for the rest of the year. If the rains come too late, young shoots are left to die in the fields, which means ruin for the peasants and famine for India! If the monsoon comes too soon, or is too violent, it turns the earth into mud and causes enormous floods that wash away everything in their path, beginning a terrible cycle of floods, desolation, and epidemics. In the rural areas, roads and bridges are cut off; in the cities, there is no electricity, and factories stop operating....

Left: Grateful for the monsoon
Right: Wheat threshing

HOW DO INDIAN PEASANTS LIVE?

Peasants in India have a hard life, and one poor harvest can plunge them into poverty. For this reason, many of them leave the country to try to make a living in the large cities....

There are around 600,000 villages in India. Seven Indians out of every ten live in the country, and men, women, and children work in the fields from morning to night. They plow the rice paddies, harvest the wheat, and look after the herds. In the past, they usually had only a wooden plow pulled by water buffalo or oxen... and no money to buy fertilizers or to dig irrigation channels. Since 1965, however, large-scale agrarian reform has improved the lot of many peasants. They are now able to own their land, instead of renting it. The state provides them with better seeds for their crops, and a special bank finances some of the work.

Today, India, which even 50 years ago could not feed its population, is now an exporter of certain foods... but three-fourths of the land is still not irrigated and farmers must depend on the monsoon for water. If there is the slightest hint of drought, the sun burns the harvests, depriving the peasants of food, of seeds for the following year, and of money with which to survive.

Although the peasants are very attached to their land, many young people can no longer tolerate this difficult existence. Every year, thousands of them sell their cattle, leave their huts, and move, with their wives and children, to try to make a living in town.

Top: Village in Rajasthan
Bottom: Young woman sorting wheat

IS IT EASY TO LIVE IN AN INDIAN CITY?

Peasants, leaving behind everything they own, flock into the big cities of India in hope of a better life.

Overpopulation is one of India's major problems. Every three years, the population increases by nearly 50 million inhabitants, resulting in many more mouths to feed, young people to educate, workers to find jobs for, families to house, sick people to care for....

The country's large cities, such as New Delhi (the capital), Bombay (the largest), and Calcutta, each have over 10 million inhabitants. Laborers—both men and women—who are lucky enough to find jobs may work for 15 hours a day in return for very little money. And they are considered lucky because they have jobs. They may be working in large factories, cotton or **jute** mills, flour mills, steelworks, and metal construction shops.

Entire Indian families are crowded into one-room apartments, without modern conveniences or plumbing, and without much hope of living better someday. But they have a roof over their heads, and they have some income—enough to feed and clothe themselves and educate their children. From the point of view of those who have nothing at all, it is better than living in the street and being forced to beg in order to survive....

Old Delhi

19

IS INDIA AS POOR AS IT IS SAID?

India is developing quickly, thanks to its universities, its scholars, its modern factories, and its tremendous capabilities. Unfortunately, the wealth is poorly distributed and the luxury of those who are better off makes the lot of the disadvantaged all the more obvious....

Many Indians in the cities as well as the country are forced to conduct "small businesses" on the sidewalk. They become candy or cigarette vendors, shoe cleaners, hot food vendors, watch repairers, tailors, barbers, and even ear cleaners! Anything is permitted, anything can be sold, and anything will do for people to earn the few rupees needed for survival until the next day. Even children must work to try to obtain the food their parents cannot always provide for them....

There are also those who are entirely without resources. In the large urban areas of India, one in every three inhabitants lives in a hut made of mud and straw, or a shed made of planks or corrugated iron. This is the shantytown, where the miserable living conditions lead to famine, epidemics, despair....

Next to this terrible poverty there is a cultured and vital elite who live in comfort. This very limited privileged class leads a nation that is eager for progress, investing in agribusiness and in the chemical, electronic, and pharmaceutical industries, building modern hospitals, laboratories, and universities, launching satellites, and mastering the atom. India is a country with a great future. It has become the tenth industrial power in the world!

Left: Modern
apartment
buildings in
Bombay
Right: Trained dog
and its young master
in the streets of Bombay

HOW DO PEOPLE TRAVEL IN INDIA?

Traveling in India is an experience that is often picturesque, rarely comfortable, and always full of unexpected events....

WOOF! WOOF!

The automobile is not much help in getting around in India. Not only are the poorly maintained roads dangerous, but the drivers of heavy trucks have no concept of safe driving. Moreover, tractor-trailers jammed full of passengers, oxcarts, camels, or elephants cause tremendous traffic congestion.

Even when traffic is not held up by a sacred cow in the middle of the road, pedestrians, bicycles, and overloaded buses prevent cars from passing. Taxis, each driver blowing his horn louder than the last, and **jinrickishas** or rickshaws, tiny two-wheeled carriages pulled by men on foot, on bicycles, or on lightweight motorcycles also contribute to the pandemonium. Ten people will squeeze onto a rickshaw seat that is a tight fit for even two adults!

Water travel is common in India. All kinds of boats travel on the rivers. For long trips, Indians generally take the train. Every large town has several huge, always crowded railroad stations. Many locomotives are still steam operated, and carriages are separated into three classes. Fares in first class, which is air-conditioned, are the same as airfares. Passengers with less money pile into the other two classes with voluminous luggage.... The trips are long—peddlers sell food and drinks in every station. Trains often run far behind schedule. Because of the slowness of rail travel, people in a hurry take a plane, or if they cannot afford that, a long-distance bus.

Left: Children going to school on a rickshaw
Right: Crowded bus

DO PEOPLE STILL RIDE ELEPHANTS IN INDIA?

Tremendously strong, but as delicate as it is docile, the elephant has always been the Indians' beast-of-all-work.

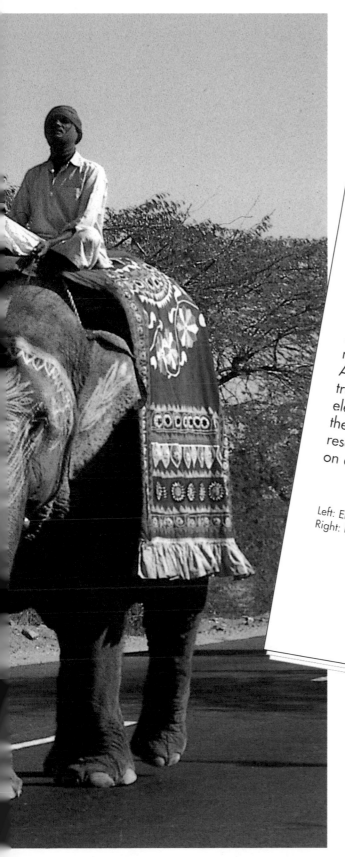

For centuries, Indian princes had their fighting elephants, the ancestors of tanks, and their show elephants for parades and festivals. Today only the temples still have one or more show elephants, used for processions. For these occasions, they are covered with ornaments and flowers.

Smaller than the African elephant, which weighs between 8,000 and 12,000 pounds and stands between nine and eleven feet tall, the Indian, or Asian, elephant weighs only about 7,000 pounds and stands between eight and nine feet tall. Its tusks are shorter, its ears are smaller, and it is humpbacked rather than swaybacked.

Elephants are still very useful in the forests as they do not need tarred roads and gas stations. The only things needed are a thicket of sugarcane and a water source.... And of course they are very useful in removing a tree trunk that has fallen across the path! Woodcutters use elephants for transporting the wood, and farmers use them for carrying or moving heavy loads. In the nature reserves, tourists get close to the wild animals by riding on an elephant's back.

Left: Elephant going to a festival
Right: Elephant for tourists

WHERE IS THE WORLD'S BIGGEST CAMEL MARKET?

In the region of Rajasthan there is a vast desert. In Pushkar, a huge camel fair takes place every year.

Every November, in Pushkar, Hindus celebrate the legend according to which Brahma, the creator-god, bathed in the city's lake. On this occasion, the inhabitants of the region come to purify themselves and take the opportunity to do their shopping—to buy or sell camels. They are indeed the most useful of animals in this desert region. At the great annual market, often over 100,000 of them are brought from all over.

Like the elephant in the Indian forests, the camel is used for just about everything. It takes the place of a tractor, a truck, and even a fast car. The female camel's milk can be consumed instead of cows' milk. A fine racing camel to be raced for sport or to be ridden by desert smugglers (so they can avoid nosy customs officials) is very expensive. The buyer will have to hand over up to 7,000 rupees!*

Top: Festival in Pushkar
Left: Decorated camel

*About $218.

23

ARE "MAN-EATING" TIGERS STILL HUNTED?

In the past, tigers terrorized Indians. There were too many tigers throughout the country, and they devoured farm animals and sometimes even human beings.

Maharajas and their distinguished guests no longer ride elephants to hunt tigers as they did at one time. Now that big game is threatened with extinction, the government has prohibited hunting them. Tigers are not the only endangered animal species. White Himalayan panthers, lions, and rhinoceros are also protected.

Because of its overpopulation, India is forced every year to level immense forests in order to farm new fields, build villages, or merely obtain wood for heating or for funeral pyres. The uncontrolled deforestation has resulted in the disappearance of the jungle where these wild animals lived, and often has catastrophic consequences, even for human beings. The earth, no longer held back by the roots of plants, is washed away by monsoon rains, and entire areas become deserts. The government has decided to intervene with the creation of huge nature reserves.

Although tigers are now reduced in numbers and kept in the reserves, they are still dangerous. If they multiply too much and if there is a shortage of game for them to eat, they attack the cows and water buffalo belonging to the peasants. When some tigers grow old and lazy, they remember the "hornless" game that does not run very fast—men! Then the decision has to be made to destroy them.

Top: Tiger
Bottom: Hunting in the jungle of Tarai

24

WHY ARE MAHARAJAHS SO ROMANTIC?

At one time, Hindu princes (the maharajas) and Muslim princes (the nabobs) governed India, exciting the imagination of foreigners by their immense wealth.

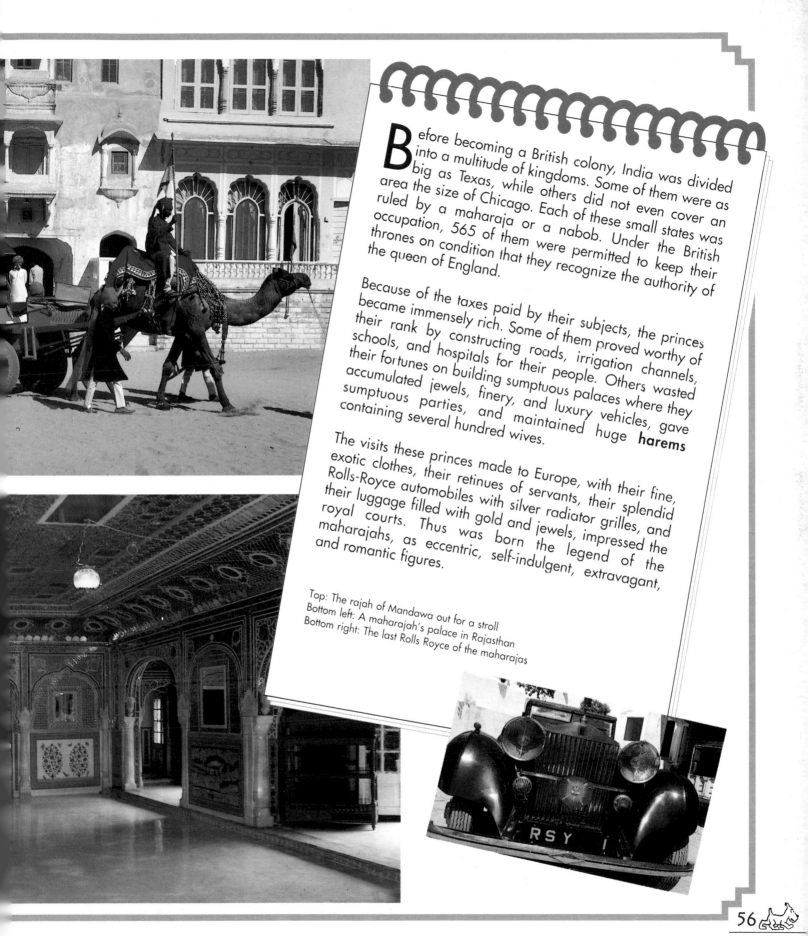

Before becoming a British colony, India was divided into a multitude of kingdoms. Some of them were as big as Texas, while others did not even cover an area the size of Chicago. Each of these small states was ruled by a maharaja or a nabob. Under the British occupation, 565 of them were permitted to keep their thrones on condition that they recognize the authority of the queen of England.

Because of the taxes paid by their subjects, the princes became immensely rich. Some of them proved worthy of their rank by constructing roads, irrigation channels, schools, and hospitals for their people. Others wasted their fortunes on building sumptuous palaces where they accumulated jewels, finery, and luxury vehicles, gave sumptuous parties, and maintained huge **harems** containing several hundred wives.

The visits these princes made to Europe, with their fine, exotic clothes, their retinues of servants, their splendid Rolls-Royce automobiles with silver radiator grilles, and their luggage filled with gold and jewels, impressed the royal courts. Thus was born the legend of the maharajahs, as eccentric, self-indulgent, extravagant, and romantic figures.

Top: The rajah of Mandawa out for a stroll
Bottom left: A maharajah's palace in Rajasthan
Bottom right: The last Rolls Royce of the maharajas

25 WHAT BECAME OF THE MAHARAJAS?

When India won its independence
in 1947 and became a republic,
the maharajas lost their kingdoms,
although they did not lose their
huge fortunes....

The splendid palaces have become museums, hotels, schools, or provincial government offices. What has become of the descendants of the former maharajas?

As in earlier times, some prefer to live in luxury and idleness, either remaining in India amid reminders of their past splendor, or emigrating to Europe or America. Others have taken advantage of their wealth and good education to become successful businessmen, ambassadors, or generals. Therefore, they continue, by serving their countries, the work of some of their ancestors, who were more concerned about the well-being of their subjects than with selfish luxury.

One the whole, even though the descendants of the maharajas are not poor, few of them allow themselves today the extravagances of former times. They understand how unwise it is to flaunt their wealth when so many Indians live in extreme poverty.

Top: Conversation among rajahs
Bottom left: Lake Palace in Udaipur
Bottom right: Palace detail

WHO WAS GANDHI?

There have always been great spiritual thinkers in India. Buddha founded a great religion; Gandhi, on the other hand, founded a nation—India.

Born in 1869, Mohandas K. Gandhi began his career as a lawyer in South Africa, a country to which many Indians had emigrated. He was incensed by the racism of the white colonists in power there. His struggle against racial segregation made him realize that violence was not an appropriate weapon in his fight for equal rights. Without ever giving up his ideals, Gandhi endured hardships and imprisonment and, in the end, his adversaries were forced to admire him.

Returning to India to carry on his struggle for independence from Great Britain, Gandhi preached a policy of "nonviolent disobedience." He was opposed to the idea of "Untouchability," and was in favor of a return to tradition, wearing as an example the cotton loincloth, or dhoti, worn by Indian peasants. Gandhi, called "Mahatma" (Great Soul) by his followers, refused to accept the social segregation of the caste system. He exhorted his followers to practice brotherhood, whether they were Hindus or Muslims, Brahmans or Pariahs, rich or poor, men or women.... After more than 30 years of his peaceful but determined struggle, India became an independent country on August 15, 1947. Gandhi lived a few months longer, respected in his own country and throughout the world. The man who India also called the "Father of the Nation" was assassinated on January 30, 1948, by a Hindu fanatic.

Gandhi

HAS INDIA ALWAYS BEEN AN INDEPENDENT COUNTRY?

India, long divided into a multitude of small kingdoms, remained a British colony for a century. It did not become independent until 1947.

In 1947, at the end of the long struggle by Gandhi and his followers, Great Britain finally granted independence to the immense colony.

The Muslims, fearing domination by the Hindus, who made up a very large majority, established a separate state called Pakistan in 1947. The Union of India is a federal republic. Among the world's democracies, it has the largest population. Indians elect their leaders and practice the religion of their choice. Pakistan, on the other hand, is a less stable country in which **Islam** is the state religion. It has experienced military dictatorship several times.

Conflicts are frequent between India and Pakistan, and war has broken out three times over Kashmir. This strategic province, where three-fourths of the population is Muslim, was given as "a gift" to the Union of India by its last maharaja, but Pakistan also claimed it.

Bangladesh (the former eastern Bengal), which broke away from Pakistan in 1971, is a small country that, while fertile, is overpopulated and very poor. Unfortunately, it is regularly ravaged by floods and hurricanes that kill hundreds of thousands of people.

The island of Ceylon, independent since 1948, became a republic in 1972 and is now called Sri Lanka. It has suffered severe economic hardship and frequent clashes of violence between Buddhists and Hindus. The Indian subcontinent now includes four countries....

Musicians and street sign in Pondicherry

28

WHY IS KASHMIR CALLED THE "GARDEN OF THE MOGULS"?

Located at the foot of the Himalayan range, Kashmir remains cool and green in the summer. For this reason, the Mogul emperors spent the hot season there, in sumptuous palaces surrounded by gardens.

Because the summers in India are intolerably hot and dry, the privileged and the powerful have always taken refuge in the mountain areas, where the weather is cool and there is still water in the rivers.

The Mogul emperors, lovers of flowers and trees, had chosen the cool valleys of Kashmir, about 500 miles (800 km) from their capital, Delhi*, as the place in which to set up their summer residence. In those days, it took at least two months to move the entire household, using elephants to carry the heavy loads. In addition to their belongings, the emperors took their court with them—their servants, their soldiers, and all their government officials.

Today, there are no emperors in New Delhi, and air-conditioning enables the leaders of modern India to tolerate the stifling heat of Indian summers in the capital. The Kashmir region still remembers the Grand Moguls who vacationed there. And the wonderful palaces of bygone days, surrounded by some of the most beautiful gardens in the world, are still there....

Left: Srinagar in Kashmir
Right: Girl in Kashmir

*The present capital is New Delhi, a new city built by the British next to the old Delhi.

29

FOR WHOM WAS THE TAJ MAHAL BUILT?

The Taj Mahal is the most famous building in India. The wonderful white marble palace is a tomb built by the Mogul Emperor Shah Jahan for his favorite wife....

In the sixteenth and seventeenth centuries, the **Moguls** established a brilliant empire in northern India, constructing some of the most beautiful monuments of Indian art, including the Taj Mahal at Agra. This splendid tomb was erected by Shah Jahan, the fourth Grand Mogul, for his adored wife Mumtaz, who died giving birth to their fourteenth child. He kept the two promises he had made to her: never to marry again and to build an imposing tomb in her memory. Work on it was begun in 1632 and it was completed 21 years later!

The architecture of the Taj is both delicate and perfectly proportioned. It is 243 feet high. Its white marble walls are incrusted with fine stones and on them are written verses from the Koran, the Muslims' sacred book. Islam had in fact become the religion of the Mogul emperors.

Many amazing stories are told about the Taj Mahal.... Shah Jahan, dethroned by one of his sons, is supposed to have spent the remainder of his life in a fortress, from whose windows he could see the tomb of his beloved, before going to rest beside her forever. Some people claim that beneath the mausoleum there is another one, an inverted replica of the Taj made of black marble, symbolizing the vanished beauty of Mumtaz. A third legend has it that Jahan had the architect of the tomb executed, so that he would never be able to build a more beautiful one. It is also said that out of regret for the crime, he planned to have a tomb built for himself, on the other side of the river, out of marble as black as sin.

Top: The Taj Mahal
Bottom: Sunset over the Taj Mahal

30 ▶ IN WHAT CITY DOES THE WIND HAVE A PALACE?

At Jaipur, in Rajasthan, there exists a palace whose tall pink facade contains 953 windows. It is known as the "Palace of the Winds."

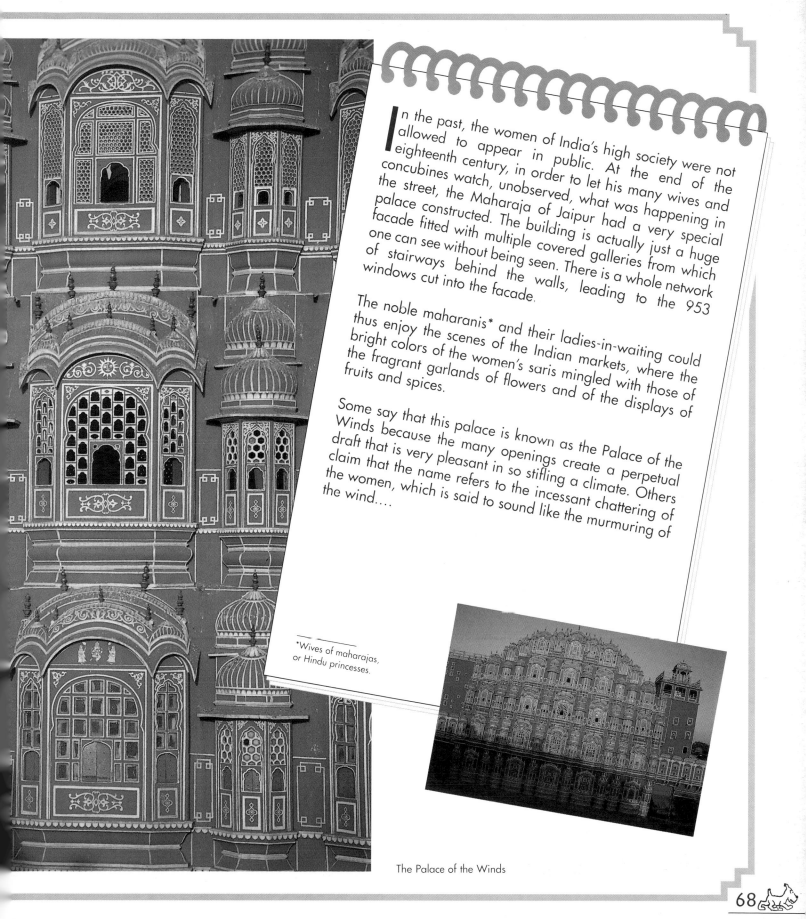

In the past, the women of India's high society were not allowed to appear in public. At the end of the eighteenth century, in order to let his many wives and concubines watch, unobserved, what was happening in the street, the Maharaja of Jaipur had a very special palace constructed. The building is actually just a huge facade fitted with multiple covered galleries from which one can see without being seen. There is a whole network of stairways behind the walls, leading to the 953 windows cut into the facade.

The noble maharanis* and their ladies-in-waiting could thus enjoy the scenes of the Indian markets, where the bright colors of the women's saris mingled with those of the fragrant garlands of flowers and of the displays of fruits and spices.

Some say that this palace is known as the Palace of the Winds because the many openings create a perpetual draft that is very pleasant in so stifling a climate. Others claim that the name refers to the incessant chattering of the women, which is said to sound like the murmuring of the wind....

*Wives of maharajas, or Hindu princesses.

The Palace of the Winds

A

ARYANS : people who invaded the north of India around 1500 B.C.; also, their language.

B

BUDDHISTS : members of a religion who practice the teachings of Buddhi that suffering is part of life and one can only be free of suffering by being pure. Buddhism appeared in northwest India around the sixth century B.C.

C

CASTE : term that, in India, indicates the divisions of society into four classes: priests, warriors, the middle classes (tradesmen, farmers, professionals), and servants.

D

DHOTI : simple white garment worn by Indian peasants; it is a type of loincloth that is wrapped between the legs to form a type of trouser.

DRAVIDIANS : earliest known inhabitants of India, they were pushed back into the southern regions by Aryan invaders around 1500 B.C.; descendants now live mainly in southern India.

H

HAREM : group of women confined to one area of a Muslim household; only male relatives were allowed to enter a harem. In the past, wealthy rulers had large harems consisting of many wives, as well as female relatives and servants.

I

ISLAM : religion preached by the Prophet Mohammed and based on the Koran (holy Muslim book); belief that there is only one God and Mohammed is His messenger.

J

JAIN : follower of Jainism, a religion practiced in India that preaches that every living thing has a soul (*jiva*) and a temporary physical body and one must avoid worldly activities in order to free the soul.

JINRICKISHA (RICKSHAW) : light two-wheeled carriage drawn by a man; used in the Far East.

JUTE : fabric made of thread that is extracted from the stem of a tropical plant; used for twine and sacking.

M

MAHARAJA : Hindu princes. *Maha* means "great" and *raja* means "king."

MOGULS : Indian dynasty founded in 1526. The deposing of the Grand Mogul by the British in 1858 marked the end of this dynasty.

MONGOL HORDES : tribes from Asia that, around the twelfth century, organized themselves into a society of conquerors. Their most important leaders were Genghis Khan and Kublai Khan.

MONSOON : system of rain-filled tropical winds in India and southern Asia that alternately blow from June to October from the sea to the land (summer monsoon) and from the land to the sea (winter monsoon). Vital to life in India because too much rain causes flooding and devastation, and too little leads to drought and famine.

MUSLIM : person who practices the religion of Muhammad, praying five times a day and traveling to their holy city, Mecca, at least once in their lives.

N

NIRVANA : literally, the "end of breathing;" designates a state of consciousness when one is free of all desire and all attachment.

P

PARSIS (PARSEES) : members of a religious community and followers of a religion originating in ancient Persia; established in western India since the eighth century A.D., it preaches good deeds.

PENINSULA : portion of land almost surrounded by water.

R

REINCARNATION : the act of rebirth; Hindus believe the soul never dies but is reborn in another form, human or animal.

S

SANSKRIT : Indo-European language that is the classical language of Brahman civilization in India.

SARI : traditional dress worn by Indian women; lightweight, approximately six-yard-long piece of fabric that hangs to the feet, with the loose end over the left shoulder; sometimes richly embroidered or jeweled.

SIKHS : followers of Sikhism; men are not permitted to cut their beards or hair; they often wear their beards rolled in a net and their hair in a knot concealed by a turban.

SUBCONTINENT : large and clearly defined portion of a continent; term is most appropriately applied to the "Indian subcontinent," which includes India, Pakistan, Bangladesh, and Sri Lanka (formerly Ceylon).

chronology

B.C.
3000

Start of the Indus civilization
Cheops has the first Giza pyramid built

2000

Aryans invade India
Israelite exodus from Egypt

1000

Beginning of the Maurya dynasty
Reign of Alexander the Great

0

Gupta Dynasty unifies India
Byzantium becomes the new capital of the Empire

500

Buddhism widespread in India
Muhammad begins preaching

1000

Conquest of northern India by Mohammed of Ghor
Beginning of the Crusades

Vasco da Gama opens the first all-water route to India from Europe
The War of the Roses

1500

Babur, descendant of Tamerlane, founds the Mogul Empire
Magellan makes first voyage around the world

1600

Founding of the British East India Company and the Dutch Netherlands India Company
Pilgrims land on Plymouth Rock; colonization begins

1700

British East India Company gains control of Bengal
American War of Independence

1800

Indian independence movement begins
American Civil War

1900
A.D.

Great Britain divides India Independence of Pakistan and of the Indian Union
World Wars I and II

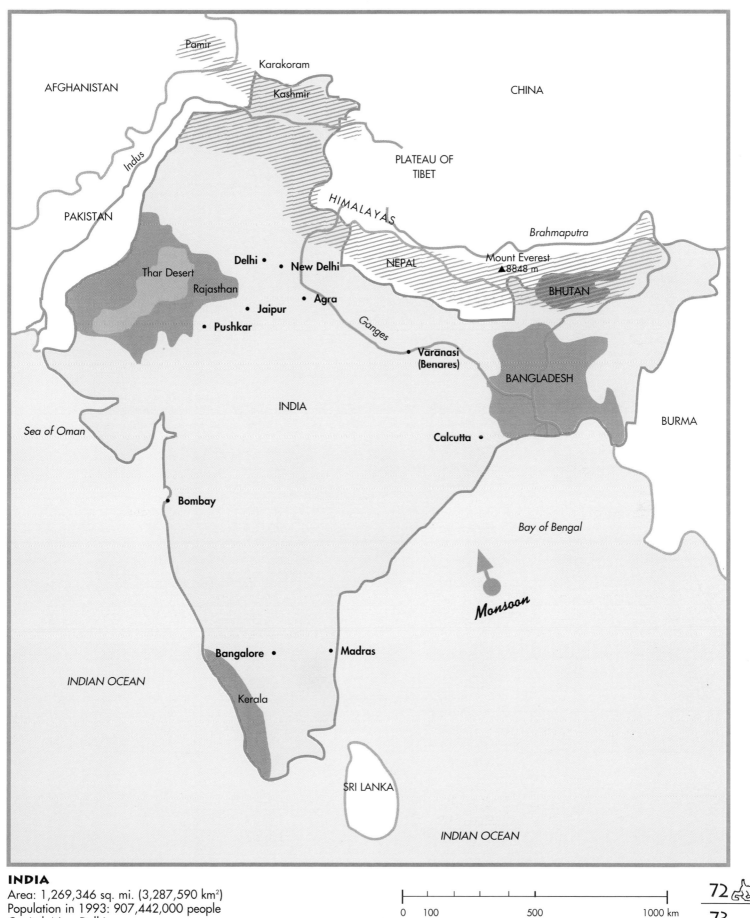

AFGHANISTAN

Pamir

Karakoram

CHINA

Kashmir

PLATEAU OF
TIBET

Indus

PAKISTAN

HIMALAYAS

Brahmaputra

Delhi • • New Delhi

NEPAL

Mount Everest
▲8848 m

Thar Desert

BHUTAN

Rajasthan

• Jaipur • Agra

Ganges

• Pushkar

Varānasi
(Benares)

BANGLADESH

INDIA

BURMA

Sea of Oman

Calcutta •

• Bombay

Bay of Bengal

Monsoon

Bangalore •

• Madras

INDIAN OCEAN

Kerala

SRI LANKA

INDIAN OCEAN

INDIA
Area: 1,269,346 sq. mi. (3,287,590 km²)
Population in 1993: 907,442,000 people
Capital: New Delhi

0   100   500   1000 km

index

Ackerley, J. R.
Hindoo Holiday: An Indian Journal.
New York: Poseidon Press, 1990.

Baker, Sophie.
Caste: At Home in Hindu India.
London: Jonathan Cape, 1990.

Blank, Jonah.
Arrow of the Blue-skinned God:
Retracing the Ramayana Through India.
Boston: Houghton Mifflin, 1992.

Brander, Michael.
The Big Game Hunters.
New York: St. Martin's Press, 1988.

Brown, Judith M.
Gandhi: Prisoner of Hope.
New Haven: Yale University Press, 1989.

Bush, Catherine.
Gandhi.
New York: Chelsea House, 1985.

Desai, Vishakha N, and Mason, Darielle, eds.
Gods, Guardians, and Lovers:
Temple Sculptures from North India.
Seattle: University of Washington Press, 1933.

Frater, Alexander.
Chasing the Monsoon.
New York: Knopf, 1991.

Gordon, Eugene.
Nepal in Pictures.
Minneapolis: The Company, 1989.

Jensen, Ann Ferguson.
India: Its Culture and People.
New York: Longman, 1991.

Kanitakara, Hemanta.
Indian Food and Drink.
New York: Bookwright Press, 1987.

Katz, Elizabeth.
India in Pictures.
Minneapolis: The Company, 1989.

Lawrence, Lady.
Indian Embers.
Palo Alto: Trackless Sands Press, 1991.

Mehta, Gita.
A Rivers Sutra.
New York: N.A. Talese, 1993.

Ramanujan, A. K., ed.
Folktales from India: A Selection of
Oral Tales from Twenty-two Languages.
New York: Pantheon Books, 1991.

Saran, Shalini.
Taj Mahal.
London: Tiger Books International, 1985.

Srinivasan, Radhika.
India. Reference ed.
New York: Marshall Cavendish, 1990.

Tillotson, G. H. R.
Mughal India.
San Francisco: Chronicle Books, 1990.

Wanasundera, Nanda.
Sri Lanka.
New York: Marshall Cavendish, 1991.

Wolpert, Stanley A.
India.
Berkeley: University of California Press, 1991.

Ummedmal Vimalkumar
INDIAN OIL DEALERS
DUDU (Raj.) 28-X-19

No. 31225   RRM 1392

Particulars	Liters	Rate	Amount Rs.	P.
H.S.D.	45	8/3	373	50
PETROL	1/2 litre		29	00
M. Oil				

Total

Cash Memo Shree R.S.T.
D.S.O. Lic. No.

Ganesh Oil Company
INDIAN OIL DEALERS
Near Balaji Temple,
Gagwana (Ajmer)
Dated

No. 8377

Particulars	Litres	Rate Rs.	Amount P.
Petrol			
H.S.D.	34	8/2	98 18
M. Oil			
Petrol with Oil			
R.R.M.			
Vehicle No. 1337			
S.T. Paid Total.			
E. & O.E.			98 18
Received Cash			

Sign

INDIANOIL

Grams : MARINA-110

Hotel Marina
NEW DELHI
G-59, CONNAUGHT CIRCUS
NEW DELHI-110001

920

TELEPHONE CHARGE SLIP
Shift Timing

8196

3.00

यात्री टिकट और सामान
जारीकर्ता

582   3425

Passenger Ticket and
ISSUED BY

इंडियन एयरलाइन्स
Indian Airlines

एयरलाइन्स हाउस, नई दिल्ली-110001
सदस्य, अंतर्राष्ट्रीय वायु परिवहन संस्था
प्रत्येक यात्री को इस टिकट की विशेष रूप से पृष्ठ 2, 3 और
4 में दी गई शर्तों की सावधानी से जाँच कर लेनी चाहिए।
धन वापसी की अवधि—जारी तिथि से दो वर्ष।
ने टिकट को सावधानी से रखिए।
पर धन की वापसी नहीं की जाती है।

Airlines House, New Delhi-110001.
Member of International Air Transport Association.
Each passenger should carefully examine
this ticket, particularly the conditions on pages 2, 3 & 4.
Refundable only within two years from date of issue.
Ensure safe custody of your ticket.
No refund is permissible against lost documents.

RESERVE BANK OF INDIA
5
पाँच रुपये
FIVE RUPEES

भारतीय रिज़र्व बैंक
2
2
ONE RUPEE

आपकी यात्रा मंगलमय हो
Wish you a happy journey

TV
L30
15

No. 8786

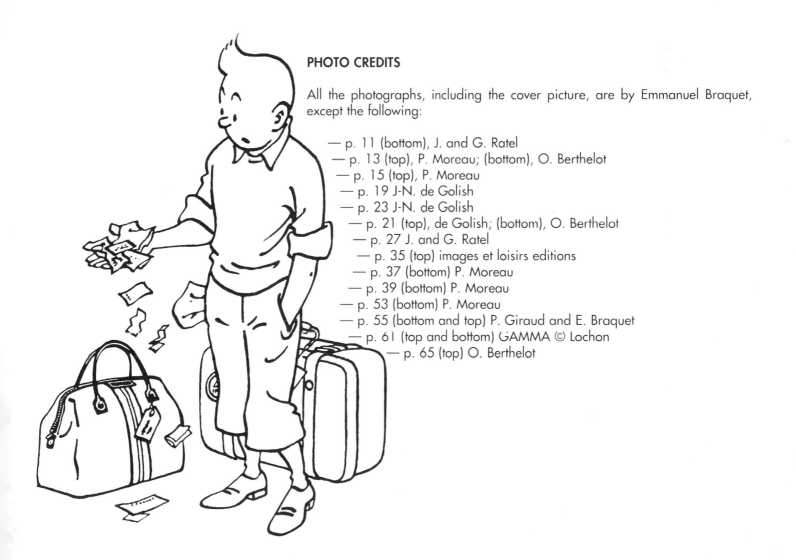

PHOTO CREDITS

All the photographs, including the cover picture, are by Emmanuel Braquet, except the following:

— p. 11 (bottom), J. and G. Ratel
— p. 13 (top), P. Moreau; (bottom), O. Berthelot
— p. 15 (top), P. Moreau
— p. 19 J-N. de Golish
— p. 23 J-N. de Golish
— p. 21 (top), de Golish; (bottom), O. Berthelot
— p. 27 J. and G. Ratel
— p. 35 (top) images et loisirs editions
— p. 37 (bottom) P. Moreau
— p. 39 (bottom) P. Moreau
— p. 53 (bottom) P. Moreau
— p. 55 (bottom and top) P. Giraud and E. Braquet
— p. 61 (top and bottom) GAMMA © Lochon
— p. 65 (top) O. Berthelot

Titles in the *Tintin's Travel Diaries* series: